for
Priscilla
Alexa and Hadley
and Frank I.
All of whom are sharing
their spiritual awakenings
with me, and allowing me
to share mine with them.

D0104668

Because of our kinship in suffering,
and because our common means of
deliverance are effective only when
constantly carried to others, our
channels of contact have always been
charged with the Language of the Heart.
— Bill W.

STEP 12

The Language of The Heart

by Peter Converse McDonald

First published March, 1983.

Copyright ©1983 by Hazelden Foundation
All rights reserved.
No part of this booklet may be reproduced
without the written permission of the publisher.
ISBN: 0-89486-167-0

Printed in the United States of America.

Editor's Note:
Hazelden Educational Materials offers a variety of information on chemical dependency and related areas. Our publications do not necessarily represent Hazelden or its programs, nor do they officially speak for any Twelve Step organization.

Introduction

Step Twelve carries us beyond ourselves to the world around us. And yet, as we go we also bring with us a great gift to give to those around us. The gift is ourselves.

In the first 11 Steps we have been primarily concerned about ourselves and our dependency. Now, in the 12th Step, we begin to reach out to others — to share ourselves with them — our stories, our thoughts, our feelings, our experiences as both dependent and recovering people. As the 12th Step tells us: "Having had a spiritual awakening as the result of these steps, we tried to carry this message to alcoholics, and to practice these principles in all our affairs."*

Our focus is now on someone else, and we place ourselves, in one way, in a secondary position. Our concern is now to help someone else recover from the disease, whether it be alcoholism or another form of chemical dependency.

But there is a paradox. We take the 12th Step as much for ourselves as for others. It is part of *our* program and no one else's. Its practice aids us in our own recovery, and ultimately it doesn't matter whether it helps anyone else.

That may sound terribly selfish, but it's true. We must always put ourselves and our recovery first — for we can be of no use to anyone else unless we do. When we do 12th Step work, if someone is helped and does get sober or does stop using, we can take some satisfaction in the fact that through us someone else has found the help he or she needed to begin recovering. We can consider it a bonus.

Just a casual reading of the 12th Step will show us that far more is involved here than helping ourselves by helping another human being. Step Twelve naturally falls into three parts which have to do with spiritual awakening, carrying the message, and practicing "these principles" (meaning the Twelve Steps).

*Alcoholics Anonymous, published by A. A. World Services, New York, NY. Available through Hazelden Educational Materials.

What follows is a guide to each of these three topics. In the first section, we will look at what it means to have a "spiritual awakening as a result of these Steps." How does it happen? How do we know a spiritual awakening is taking place? What's it like to awaken spiritually?

In the second section, we will consider different ways of "carrying this message." How do we go about making a 12th Step call? Are there different kinds? What "message" are we carrying? When can we start doing 12th Step work? Do we have to wait until we've made at least a start on the other 11 Steps?

In the final section, we will focus on using the 12 Steps "in all our affairs," not just applying them to our disease. How can these Steps be used in our relationships, on the job, at home? Again, Step 12 is taking us beyond ourselves and our chemical dependency to other people and situations. We may be surprised to find how helpful the 12 Steps are when applied to "all our affairs." In a very real way, they become a way of life. Applied to all areas of our lives, the 12 Steps can bring us to a joy of living.

"Having had a spiritual awakening as the result of these steps . . ."

Just exactly what is a spiritual awakening, and how do we know when we are waking up spiritually?

The opening words of Step 12 imply that a spiritual awakening is something which has occurred in the past, and is now completed. But it's important to realize that such an awakening is an ongoing, never-ending *process*. It may have begun sometime in the past when we took the First Step, but it continues for the rest of our lives. It is not a distinct event with a clear beginning and ending. That is the first thing to remember about spiritual awakenings.

The second is that every person's spiritual awakening is unique, that no two are exactly alike. But that doesn't mean that each is not just as real and valid.

However, spiritual awakenings have some common denominators. They often follow long periods of mental or emotional darkness. We may have felt terribly alone, as if no one understood us.

Spiritual awakenings are often described as just that, awakenings. They represent a coming to conscious awareness of ourselves as we really are, an awareness of a power greater than ourselves which may be outside ourselves, or deep within ourselves, or both. Where there was darkness, now there is light. We can see things more realistically. Indeed we can see things we never saw before. Most people experience a sense of letting go. But in addition, many of us, especially women, report a gaining of power, a coming to our true selves after surrenduring. There is a sense of grounding of ourselves in a power we didn't know before.

I like to think of spiritual awakening in terms of waking up in the morning. The process seems to start before we are conscious and awake. We may start to toss and turn in our sleep. We may dream. We may become uncomfortable, stiff, too hot or too cold. We sometimes open one eye and check to see what the weather is, then groan and fall back asleep for a few minutes. But we're starting to wake up.

Then the alarm goes off, and we're at least somewhat awake. We know we are conscious. We can see the room around us and ourselves sitting sleepily on the edge of the bed.

The beginning of recovery is like that — the beginning of our spiritual awakening. We toss and turn, become very uncomfortable, perhaps very ill or very separated from our families and friends in some way. We groan, turn over, and go back to sleep, denying that there is anything wrong with us, not yet willing to face the reality of ourselves and our condition. We put our heads under the pillow, trying to keep out the light of day that will make it clear to us that we have a problem, that we're powerless

3

over alcohol or other drugs and that our lives are unmanageable. We fight to stay asleep spiritually.

But the alarm has, indeed, gone off. Perhaps some crisis forces us to wake up, to see ourselves as we really are. There may be an intervention by our families or employers. Or in a rare moment of insight, we may realize that we have a problem and need help. But one way or another, when the alarm goes off, we admit we are powerless. Our spiritual awakening has begun.

Once we are awake, how do we know the process is continuing? What are some of the signs that tell us we're making spiritual progress?

Probably the most practical way to tell is to look at our behavior. Is it any different than it was in the past, before we began waking up? To continue the metaphor of getting up in the morning, are we now getting out of bed right away, rather than hitting the snooze alarm for a few more minutes of sleep? Are we eager for the day ahead? If so, that's a sign of spiritual progress.

Other examples of changing behavior: do we procrastinate less? Are we getting things done more quickly? Do we admit our mistakes more readily, both to ourselves and to others? Can we even laugh about them a little bit? Are we asking for help when we need it, rather than being stubborn and thinking we don't need help? Are we more open and honest about our shortcomings? Do we accept them as part of who we are? Are we beginning to claim the good parts of ourselves? Are we more willing to let go of our resentments towards others? Do we make amends when we hurt someone else, sincerely admitting we were wrong? On a daily basis, are we more aware of our behavior and attitudes? Do we find ourselves taking time each day to be quiet, perhaps to meditate or to pray? Are we reaching out to help others who may need us?

If the answer to any one of those questions is "yes," then we can say that we are waking up spiritually. And that our spiritual awakening continues.

No doubt you've noticed that the foregoing is a review of some of the 12 Steps from a behavioral point of view. The point is that if we are working the Steps, using them in our daily lives in order to stay sober or chemically free, then we are certainly making spiritual progress. And it's important to remember that we don't have to be working all of the Steps every day in order to be making progress. One is enough, for starters. But as our awakening continues, we'll probably find that we're using more and more of the Steps on a daily basis.

The behavior of others may also indicate to us that we are making progress on a spiritual level. Are our spouse and children more trusting of us? Have we regained some respect from them, or from fellow employees and friends? Are we given more responsibilty at work or at home? If so, it's probably because those around us see some positive changes in us. They may see spiritual progress that we haven't noticed until they illuminate it by their new trust and respect.

However, my own experience as a recovering person reminds me that the regaining of trust and responsibility and respect, especially from our spouses, may happen very slowly. After all, I was a pretty sick person for a long time, and I had to prove — by my own behavior — that I could be trusted by my wife. She put up with my drinking and bizarre behavior for years, and it has taken years for her to trust me again. So I had to be patient with her, as patient as she was with me. The point is that we need not be hurt or disappointed if we don't immediately receive the respect and trust we want.

What are some other ways of knowing that we're awakening spiritually? One is that we may have experiences which can be called spiritual.

A spiritual *experience* is very different from the ongoing spiritual *awakening*. It is an event that has a distinct beginning and end. That's a crucial distinction. Some of us used to think that if we had such an experience, we were "converted" or "born again," or that suddenly we "got it" and were "healed." We thought that was all there was to it. That's not the case. Spiritual experiences are merely signs along the way that we're making progress in our spiritual awakening.

Spiritual experiences come in many different forms, and not everyone has them. Although rare, some are very dramatic. Most seem to be subtle. Spiritual experiences can be, and usually are, common, everyday events which, in our new sobriety, we now see as having a spiritual element to them. And like spiritual awakenings, spiritual experiences also can be unique to the person.

What are some examples of spiritual experiences which will tell us we're making progress? The dramatic type is the one that comes to mind first. Sometimes it can happen right at the beginning of our spiritual awakening, although that's rare. One person I know said he suddenly had a visual replay of all his drinking life and behavior — in the course of just a few seconds — and realized he was alcoholic. He then went and got help. He called it "enlightenment," and for him it was not only a spiritual experience, but a mystical one as well.

Probably the rest of us may have to be content with less amazing circumstances. My own spiritual experiences usually take me by surprise. They're ordinary events like watching the sun go down over a lake, seeing a smile on a baby's face, listening to good music, and the like.

Spiritual experiences can also be moments of insight when we say to ourselves, "Aha! Of course. I'd never made that connection before, but I see it clearly now." You know the feeling — when something suddenly falls into place for you and is obvious to you. That's a spiritual experience — for me, anyway. Others may choose to interpret it differently.

Such experiences are not always positive ones at the time. In fact, sometimes they can be very painful. It's only in retrospect that one can look at them as being spiritual in nature.

For instance, I once had to end a relationship with a woman I loved very much. Both of us had invested a great deal of ourselves in the relationship, and both of us had tried very hard to make it work. But after a time it became clear that we were not compatible people, and so we mutually agreed to part.

The last time I saw her was excruciatingly painful. We finally had nothing left to say to each other, and so we hugged and said good-bye. I knew she was crying as she turned away to go, and I wondered why I wasn't. I just felt numb, empty. A little later, I went to a place that is very special to me — to be alone, to cry, to do whatever I had to do. I found myself talking to my Higher Power, asking why this had to happen, why all my hopes and dreams and plans had been destroyed. In fact, I got very angry with my Higher Power. I did a lot of yelling and swearing. I also got angry at her for not being the person I wanted her to be. Finally, I got angry at myself because I couldn't make the relationship work. I was powerless. Then I cried, not just a few sniffles, but huge racking sobs that seemed to come from the deepest part of me.

Afterwards, I felt empty again. But something was different. Some of the heaviness was gone. There was some peace, some acceptance of the fact that the relationship was ended, perhaps even some serenity.

Even though it was terribly painful, that hour or so was a spiritual experience for me. Why? Because I was very aware of my God's presence within me, because I was very aware of myself and how much I was hurting, and how much my friend apparently had been hurting.

I think that is a common denominator to all spiritual experiences, no matter how large or small the experiences may be. In all of them there is some awareness of Another, of a

Higher Power, a Greater Good, a Deeper Self, a God within or without. However it is for you, such an awareness is found in every spiritual experience.

And that's what tells us we are making progress spiritually, that our spiritual awakening is continuing. It's the fact that every once in awhile, we are aware of some other Power operating in our lives, sometimes in us or in other people, sometimes in nature, and sometimes in common, everyday occurrences.

"...we tried to carry this message to alcoholics..."

Here is the heart of the 12th Step. This is what it's really all about. "Carrying the message" means that we reach out to other alcoholics or chemically dependent people and tell them the story of our own spiritual awakening. That is the message we carry: that as a result of the Steps, we came to awaken spiritually, began to recover, and continue to do so. It is a message of hope.

We take the 12th Step for two reasons. The first and primary one is to strengthen our own recovery, to continue our own spiritual growth by sharing ourselves with another human being. Something happens to us when we do that. There is value in giving of ourselves. We always receive something back, whether it's new strength or new self-insight, the satisfaction of attempting to help another person, or the realization that someone else needs us, that we have something of value to share. That something of value is ourselves.

The second reason for taking the 12th Step is that by doing so, others may come to awaken spiritually. In our story, they may see some hope for themselves, for they may identify with part of our story. Perhaps the circumstances of our drinking or using may be similar to theirs. They may say to themselves, "Well, if that person can do it, can stop using or drinking, then just maybe so can I."

Step 12 is called "the language of the heart" because that's exactly what it is. When we take the 12th Step and talk with someone else, we are talking from our hearts. We're being as honest and as open as we can about who we are, where we've been, and how we got to where we are today in terms of our recovery and spiritual growth.

Those of us who are recovering have found many different methods of taking the 12th Step. But in every method, we share at least a part of ourselves — whether it's by telling some or all of our story, by giving our time or energy to help someone else, or by serving others in some way.

When can we start to take the 12th Step? Are there any special qualifications we need, any special training? To answer the first question, if we have taken Step One, if we've been through treatment, or if we've been to a meeting, then we've already done 12th Step work. As to the second question, the only qualification necessary is the ability to tell our stories as honestly as we can. No special training is needed. Being ourselves is enough.

Just by our presence at a meeting, without saying a word, we are helping the other people at the meeting by sharing ourselves. Being there is a way to share ourselves, perhaps even the best way. And when we do speak, even if it's only to smile and say hello to a newcomer at the meeting, we are working the 12th Step. It's as simple as that.

Traditionally, 12th Step work has been done by visiting with another individual who is perceived as needing help, in order to help him or her awaken spiritually and begin the process of recovery. That individual usually is still drinking or using and can't see the reality of his or her behavior and its effects on other people. Such visits can be at the request of the person's family, or by personal request. The visit is made because we see a problem with a friend or relative, and we want to help if we can. These visits are generally known as 12th Step "calls."

In addition, there are many other ways of doing 12th Step work as part of our program of recovery. Doing volunteer work at a treatment center is one method. Volunteering to spend time answering phones at A.A. Central Service is another. Visiting with patients in detox clinics or with residents in a halfway house are two more. And some recovering alcoholics and chemically dependent people leave their names and phone numbers with A.A. Central Service in their city, so if someone calls and wants help, A.A. will have helpers available.

Some of us who are recovering also may be asked to participate in an "intervention." That, too, is a form of 12th Step work. In those cases we usually know the person well, and vice versa, either because we are a member of the family, a close friend, or a fellow employee. Interventions are generally carried out with the help or advice of a professionally trained counselor. They serve to confront a person with the reality of his or her drinking/using behavior, after which the person is usually asked to make a choice as to what s/he wishes to do. Usually the choice is clear, but sometimes it is painful. Either the person seeks help in some way (through treatment or going to A.A., for instance), or s/he will lose his or her job, or the spouse will ask for a separation. Whatever the situation or circumstance, in all 12th Step work we share ourselves by telling our story: how we came to be dependent, what it was like for us, how we came to be sober or chemically free, and how our spiritual awakening took place.

In 12th Step work it's often appropriate to make observations about the behavior of the person we are trying to help. In such cases, it's important to report only the facts of the behavior that we have observed and to do so in a caring and non-judgmental way. That way, the person we are trying to help will not be put on the defensive.

However, usually all we have to do is to tell our story. By so doing we are holding up a mirror to others as if to say, "Look, this is what happened to me. Do you see any of yourselves in here, in my story?" That is another way of presenting the reality of their own drinking/using behavior in a manner they may be able to accept. It is less confrontive and less threatening than directly pointing out their own behavior. It is a way of saying to them that it's okay to be the way I was and the way they are now.

Through painful trial and error, those of us who have done 12th Step work have developed a set of guidelines or suggestions. Those guidelines help us to be more effective in terms of transmitting the message and encouraging the recipient to ask for our help. What follows are not hard and fast rules. But I know they help make 12th Step work more effective and less frustrating for those of us who make 12th Step calls.

1) Make 12th Step calls with another person. Don't try to do one by yourself. One reason is the person you're visiting with will then have double the chance to identify with one of the two stories he or she is hearing. Another, more practical reason for taking someone with you is for self-protection. The person on whom you are calling may be drunk and may become violent. By the time you get there, he or she may be passed out. If the person agrees to get help and you need to provide transportation, it's a good idea to have someone in the car with you. Have your partner sit in the back seat with the person you are helping.

2) If you are calling on a person of the opposite sex, take someone of that same sex with you. If you're a man calling on a woman, she has a ready-made excuse for not identifying with you because you're not a woman. But if you have a woman with you, she won't have that excuse. Indeed, she may be able to see some of herself in your partner's story.

3) Tell your own story. Stick to it and be as honest and specific as you can. Talk about what your behavior was like when you were drinking or using, what you did and what you

said. Tell how much you drank or used and how it affected you. Tell how you felt about yourself when you were drinking or using. Tell how it affected your family, your job. The more you say, the better the person will be able to identify with at least part of your story.

Then talk about your own recovery. Tell how it started. Tell when and how you started to awaken spiritually, although you need not use that phrase, especially if you know the person would have a problem with it. Talk about what finally made you admit that you were powerless and that your life was indeed unmanageable. If you went to treatment, talk about what it was like. If someone took you to a meeting, tell what that was like. Talk about what your life has been like since. Be honest about that, too. For instance, my own life hasn't been all peaches and cream since I took the First Step, but it's much better than it was when I was drinking.

4) Offer help because you care and you want to, not just because you think the person needs it (even if it's obvious to you that he or she does.) The person may even ask your advice on what to do. In that case, try to act as a facilitator in the decision-making. You can do that by listing the various options you know and by making a recommendation.

5) Have no expectations. The person may decide to continue drinking or using. In fact, that is usually the case. It's important to know that so we aren't disappointed or upset because the person has not responded to our story and offer of help. We can take solace in the fact that we did our best. We planted a seed of thought. The person we visited knows where to get help. We also know that we have succeeded in a big way because we have taken the 12th Step as part of our own program of recovery. We have done something for ourselves which is helping us to stay sober or chemically free.

6) If the person does accept our help, be prepared to follow

through. That may mean taking him or her to a meeting, arranging for admission to a treatment center or outpatient program, or even providing transportation to a treatment center. If treatment is the decision, stay in touch by phone or letter. Let the person know you care and are standing by. When treatment concludes, offer to take him or her to meetings. We know what it was like at the beginning of recovery and how much we appreciated people who cared about us.

7) Perhaps more important than anything else, always show both care and respect for the person you are calling. Being judgmental won't do any good, and as recovering people ourselves, we have no right to be judgmental. We know about denial, for instance. And we know the person we are visiting is deserving of our concern and respect simply because he or she is a human being, like us, and who may be very ill. So it's important not to let the other person sense any impatience or anger or judgment in us. Such feelings are entirely out of place in a 12th Step visit — and certainly are not good for our own recovery process. In fact, they are signs that we still have work to do on ourselves. But if we have enough respect for the person to let him or her be, and if we can remember that we can only change ourselves and no one else (I've often said the Serenity Prayer silently while on a 12th Step call), we will make it much easier for that person to request and accept our help.

These are just a few general suggestions which can be applied to any kind of 12th Step work. As you gain experience, you will discover what works and what doesn't for you, and you'll develop your own guidelines.

"...and to practice these principles in all our affairs."

"These principles" mean the 12 Steps. "Affairs" mean all aspects of our daily lives.

Until now, we have been concerned primarily with getting

sober or straight. We've been using the 12 Steps to do that. We've admitted that we are powerless over alcohol and that our lives had become unmanageable because of our drinking or using. But as we gain some sobriety, we begin to realize that it isn't just alcohol or drugs over which we're powerless, but over many other things, as well. We begin to see we are powerless over our spouses, children, friends, and colleagues at work. We begin to see that we have no control over their behavior or thoughts or attitudes or feelings. We can't make them do or say or feel what we want. If we try, we know our lives will become unmanageable again.

Of course, it would be wonderful if our wife or husband loved and trusted us as perhaps they once did. But we can't make them do so. We have no control over their feelings. So what do we do? We believe that a Power greater than ourselves will restore us to sanity, and we turn the problem over to that Power. We let go, using Step 3.

Perhaps our supervisor at work isn't giving us the raise we want, or more responsibility in our job. We could choose to get angry and resentful, or to feel sorry for ourselves. But would that do any good? The alternative is to turn over our resentment or self-pity (Step 7) and get on with our job. Perhaps if we work hard enough, we will gain the supervisor's respect, and then we'll get that raise or increased responsibility. Perhaps not. But by going back to Step 1, we realize we are powerless over our supervisor and his or her attitude towards us. All we can change is ourselves. In the end, we may have to consider a different job where we might get the respect we feel we deserve.

In the course of our 4th and 5th Steps, we may have discovered that one of our character defects is impatience (certainly, it's one of mine). In our daily lives, what can we do about it? If our husband or wife is continually late, do we still get impatient, or are we beginning to learn how to let go and let him or her be late? Can we find something constructive to do instead of just waiting impatiently? If so, we're practicing the Steps in another aspect of our daily lives.

In this case, Step 1 helps us realize we are powerless over our spouse's actions. In Step 3 we turn it over, in Step 4 we identify our impatience, and in Step 7 we let go of the impatience. In Step 9 we tell our spouse we've been impatient with him or her and apologize, making amends. In Step 10 we continue to monitor our behavior and attitudes on a daily basis to see if we're becoming more patient. In Step 11 we may pray or meditate on what our Higher Power wills for us in regard to our spouse, his or her lateness, and our impatience. And in Step 12, we may find a way to help our spouse be on time, perhaps by sharing how we used to be late all the time and how we came to be on time. Perhaps then our spouse may change his or her behavior. Or we can change our own behavior, quit waiting, and let our latecomer eat alone.

That may be an overly simplistic example of how the 12 Steps can be applied in an everyday situation of our lives, but it illustrates how it can be done. And when it is, it makes life much easier to live.

If we use the 12 Steps in all our affairs, as the 12th Step suggests, we will find ourselves truly changed people. We will find new serenity. We will be selfless people, honestly caring about our families and friends. We will be more understanding, less critical, more giving of ourselves. And we will receive the love and care and trust and respect that we know we deserve when we are living our lives to the best of our abilities.

Obviously, it is asking too much of ourselves to demand that we practice all the Steps all the time. I know I don't. But we can make a start. We can want to do the best we can.

As I go about my 12th Step work, carrying the message and practicing the 12 Steps as best I can in all my affairs, I often think of the prayer attributed to St. Francis of Assisi. I've adopted it as my 12th Step prayer.

God, make us instruments of your peace.
Where there is hatred, let us sow love;
where there is injury, pardon;
where there is discord, union;
where there is doubt, faith.
where there is despair, hope;
where there is darkness, light;
where there is sadness, joy.
Grant that we may not so much
seek to be consoled as to console;
to be understood as to understand;
to be loved, as to love.
For it is in pardoning that we are pardoned;
and it is in dying that we are born
to eternal life.

(from the Episcopal Book of Common Prayer, 1979)